RACIAL JUSTICE IN AMERICA

What Are
MY RIGHTS?

We The

People

KELISA WING

CHERRY LAKE PRESS

Published in the United States of America by Cherry Lake Publishing Group
Ann Arbor, Michigan
www.cherrylakepublishing.com

Reading Adviser: Marla Conn, MS, Ed., Literacy specialist, Read-Ability, Inc.
Content Adviser: Kelisa Wing
Book Design and Cover Art: Felicia Macheske

Photo Credits: © Rawpixel.com/Shutterstock.com, 6, 27; Library of Congress Control No.: 2003675329, 9; Library of Congress/Photograph by Warren K. Leffeler, LOC Control No.: 2014645538, 10; Library of Congress/Photograph by Marion S. Trikosko, LOC Control No.: 2013647403, 12; © Everett Collection/Shutterstock.com, 13; © Sundry Photography/Shutterstock.com, 14; © a katz/Shutterstock.com, 17; © VDB Photos/Shutterstock.com, 19; © Craig Chaddock/Shutterstock.com, 21; Library of Congress/Photograph by Dick DeMarsico, LOC Control No.: 99404328, 22; © Helder Almeida/Shutterstock.com, 25; © Joseph Sohm/Shutterstock.com, 30; © steve estvanik/Shutterstock.com, 31

Graphics Throughout: © debra hughes/Shutterstock.com; © GoodStudio/Shutterstock.com; © Natewimon Nantiwat/Shutterstock.com; © Galyna_P/Shutterstock.com

Library of Congress Cataloging-in-Publication Data

Names: Wing, Kelisa, author.
Title: What are my rights? / Kelisa Wing.
Description: Ann Arbor, Michigan : Cherry Lake Publishing, 2021. | Series:
    Racial justice in America | Includes index. | Audience: Grades 4-6 |
    Summary: "Race in America has been avoided in children's education for too long.
    What Are My Rights? explores the right you have in school, activism, and with the police
    in a comprehensive, honest, and age-appropriate way. Developed in conjunction with educator,
    advocate, and author Kelisa Wing to reach children of all races and encourage them to approach
    race issues with open eyes and minds. Includes 21st Century Skills and content, as well as a PBL
    activity across the Racial Justice in America series. Also includes a table of contents, glossary, index,
    author biography, sidebars, educational matter, and activities"— Provided by publisher.
Identifiers: LCCN 2020039991 (print) | LCCN 2020039992 (ebook)
    | ISBN 9781534180246 (hardcover) | ISBN 9781534181953 (paperback)
    | ISBN 9781534181250 (pdf) | ISBN 9781534182967 (ebook)
Subjects: LCSH: Civil rights—United States—Juvenile literature. | Social justice—United States—
    Juvenile literature. | United States—Race relations—Juvenile literature.
Classification: LCC JC599.U5 W56 2021 (print) | LCC JC599.U5 (ebook) |
    DDC 323.0973—dc23
LC record available at https://lccn.loc.gov/2020039991
LC ebook record available at https://lccn.loc.gov/2020039992

Cherry Lake Publishing Group would like to acknowledge the work of the Partnership for 21st Century Learning, a Network of Battelle for Kids. Please visit *http://www.battelleforkids.org/networks/p21* for more information.

Printed in the United States of America
Corporate Graphics

For Naima and Jadon

Kelisa Wing honorably served in the U.S. Army and has been an educator for 14 years. She is the author of *Promises and Possibilities: Dismantling the School to Prison Pipeline, If I Could: Lessons for Navigating an Unjust World,* and *Weeds & Seeds: How to Stay Positive in the Midst of Life's Storms.* She speaks both nationally and internationally about discipline reform, equity, and student engagement. Kelisa lives in Northern Virginia with her husband and two children.

CHAPTER 1

Introduction to Your Rights

You may have heard that you have the right to "life, liberty, and the pursuit of happiness." This phrase comes from the Declaration of Independence, a document created in 1776 by our nation's Founding Fathers. The rights promised in this document are inalienable. The Bill of Rights, the first 10 amendments of the U.S. Constitution, gives Americans additional rights, including the rights to freedom of speech, press, and assembly.

These freedoms are promised to our citizens through documents created at our nation's birth. All people are legally, morally, and socially entitled to them.

Fifty-six men signed the Declaration of Independence. John Hancock's

While it's important to have documents that establish rights, it's equally important to have rules in place to protect those rights. Over the years, we have passed laws to **prohibit discrimination** on the basis of race, age, **gender**, and ability. However, some would say we still have a long way to go.

Discrimination is a violation of our inalienable rights.

What does all of this mean for you as a student? It means you have a right to speak your mind in school, a right to express yourself through speech, and a right to a free public education. You have these rights no matter what your race, religion, gender, or national origin is.

Your rights matter. Understanding your rights will help you as a student and as you continue to learn and grow.

Critical Thinking

Did you know that rules in your school cannot interfere with the rights you have? What are the rules in your school? What would you do to speak up and speak out against rules that violate your rights? For example, does your dress code go against your rights? Are there rules that target girls or boys specifically?

CHAPTER 2

History of Rights in America

Today, many people are concerned about their rights when it comes to equal treatment, voting, protest, and free speech. We understand that we all have rights, but how did they come to be? Let's look at the history of some of the movements that gave us those rights and paved the way for the protests of today.

In 1848, a group of activists in Seneca Falls, New York, gathered to discuss fighting for the right of women to vote. At the time, only White men could vote. This meeting was called the Seneca Falls Convention. In 1869, Susan B. Anthony and Elizabeth Cady Stanton founded the National Woman Suffrage Association to fight for an amendment to the U.S. Constitution that would give women the vote. The group merged with a second group in 1890 and became the National American Woman Suffrage Association. It took many years of fighting for their rights, but in 1920, the 19th Amendment was added to the Constitution. Women could now vote in all elections.

The women's suffrage movement worked for more than 70 years before achieving their goal.

For Black people in America, it took much longer to gain true rights of equality. The 15th Amendment had granted Black men the right to vote in 1870. But Jim Crow laws had already begun. These racist laws forced Black people to drink from separate water fountains, attend segregated schools, and use separate restrooms. In addition, these laws were taking away the rights promised by the 15th Amendment.

Jim Crow laws made it difficult for Black people to vote in national and local elections—and were a violation of rights.

Events of the 1950s and 1960s caused the calls for civil rights to grow louder. Emmett Till, a Black 14-year-old, was brutally murdered in Mississippi for supposedly flirting with a White woman. Rosa Parks refused to give up her seat on an Alabama bus to a White man. And the Black students who became the Little Rock Nine bravely tried to attend a White high school in Arkansas. After years of protests, marches, and demonstrations, the Civil Rights Act of 1964 was finally signed into law. This outlawed discrimination and enforced desegregation. The next year, the Voting Rights Act of 1965 became law, giving Black people equal voting rights and protections from racist voting rules.

Take a virtual tour of the National Museum of African American History and Culture by visiting *https://nmaahc.si.edu*. There are 35,000 artifacts that tell the story of Black people in America. After visiting, think about what else you learned about the history of rights.

The March on Washington

Have you ever felt helpless? What did you do in that moment? Did you quit or keep going? During the civil rights era, people who felt helpless not only kept going, but they also marched! The March on Washington was held on the National Mall in 1963 and drew over 250,000 people. Congressman John Lewis was the youngest person to speak at the march. He was just 23! He was the last living speaker from that day until he died on July 17, 2020. What other facts can you find out about John Lewis and the March on Washington?

Martin Luther King Jr. delivered his famous "I Have a Dream" speech at the March on Washington.

What is gerrymandering? Look online to find out. How does gerrymandering interfere with fair elections?

The legal rights that let all Americans vote safely and expect equal education and treatment under the law were the result of activists who were willing to speak up and speak out for what is right and fair. And their fight isn't over. Civil rights and voting rights are always under attack. Discrimination is still a problem.

Talk to a teacher about where they still see unfairness under the law. Think about the rights and treatment of Black people, members of the LGBTQ communities, and women.

CHAPTER 3

Current Action

Many people are still fighting for what is right and fair today. Protesting is one of the best ways to get your voice heard. And the right to protest is protected by the U.S. Constitution. There are two reasons why people protest.

One reason is because people feel strongly about something. An example is when student activists organized March for Our Lives in March 2018 following the mass shooting at Marjory Stoneman Douglas High School. The protest was the largest against gun violence in history. The students turned this single event into an organization that would help people get registered to vote, learn about their rights, and end gun violence. Another example of people protesting for or against something they feel strongly about is climate change. People are fighting for climate change by promising to recycle, carpool, call their government officials, and buy things that are better for the environment.

In 2014, more than 300,000 people marched in New York City's People's Climate March.

People also protest to fight for their rights or the rights of others. The Black Lives Matter movement (BLM) is an example of this type of protest. BLM began in 2013 in response to the mistreatment of Black people and the murder of Trayvon Martin. Today, the movement is dedicated to the freedom of Black people to live without racism.

After the murder of George Floyd in Minneapolis in May 2020, there were BLM protests in over 2,000 cities and 60 countries. Protesters called for racial justice and demanded an end to the mistreatment of people of color in America. The protests in 2020 were the largest in U.S. history.

Do you ever think you are too young to be heard? It is important for you to know that you have rights and you are never too young to make a difference! Eight-year-old Nolan Davis realized this when in June 2020 he organized a Children's Black Lives Matter March in Minnesota. In what ways can you use your voice to make a difference?

"Injustice anywhere is a threat to justice everywhere" means that even if a particular injustice doesn't directly effect you, the fact that it exists puts you and your rights at risk.

Another example of protesting to work for the rights of others is the fight in 2020 for equal voting rights. Congressman John Lewis worked tirelessly for voting rights his whole life. After he died in July 2020, people asked the U.S. Congress to address problems involving mail-in voting, absentee voting, and voter suppression.

What other issues do you see people in your community protesting against?

Life as a Reporter

Learning about the backgrounds of others is the best way to eliminate racism. Find a friend in class who has a different background than you. Research their nationality, race, and traditions by interviewing them. Understanding more about the people around us allows us to see that we are all, as Martin Luther King Jr. said, "human and therefore brothers."

year. Congress simply did not have enough money to pay for a war against the greatest military power in the world.

Soon after Washington wrote his letter, he received word that a large British force had landed in Charleston, South Carolina. A month later, that port fell, and British troops began taking control of key southern areas.

The French Arrive

As the summer of 1780 arrived, Washington finally received some encouraging news. In July, a large, well-trained force of 5,000 French troops under General Jean-Baptiste-Donatien de Vimeur, Comte de Rochambeau, arrived in Newport, Rhode Island. The force was small, but it was experienced, highly disciplined, and well armed.

On September 22, 1780, Washington met Rochambeau for the first time in Hartford, Connecticut, halfway between the two armies. The American commander proposed an all-out attack on New York City, but those plans were never developed.

On September 25, Washington received disturbing news. General Benedict Arnold, the hero of the American victory at Saratoga in 1777—the triumph that convinced France to aid the United States—had gone over to the British side. Arnold left his command at West Point and fled to New York City, where Clinton offered him a commission as a general in His Majesty's Army.

9

The French force of 5,000 men, including a large cavalry unit, landed in Rhode Island in the summer of 1780.

In December 1780, Clinton put Arnold in command of a 6,000-man British force and sent the troops by ship to Virginia. Throughout early 1781, Arnold created chaos in the eastern region of the state. He and his men burned tobacco warehouses and even drove Virginia's governor, Thomas Jefferson, into hiding.

As 1781 arrived, Washington faced disasters in both North and South. In January, the Pennsylvania militia stationed in northern New Jersey staged a mutiny and killed their commanding officer. The troops set out to Philadelphia to demand payment from Congress. Within weeks, the New Jersey militia also mutinied. Washington was forced to devote much of his time to preventing the complete breakdown of the Continental forces. Eventually, the mutinies were defeated, and Washington ordered the execution of several Americans for their part in the revolt.

The War in the South

Throughout the spring and summer of 1780, while Washington was absorbed with military matters in the North, much of the fighting between the British and American armies took place in the South. Clinton led a British force south to Charleston. Like many British military leaders, he believed that there was strong Loyalist sentiment in the South, especially among the large plantation owners whose cotton and tobacco had been sold to England before the war. At first, he had great success in forming a large Loyalist militia unit among southern colonists.

In Charleston, American regular troops and Patriot militia held out against Clinton's army for a month before they surrendered. Afterward, a British captain who observed the American

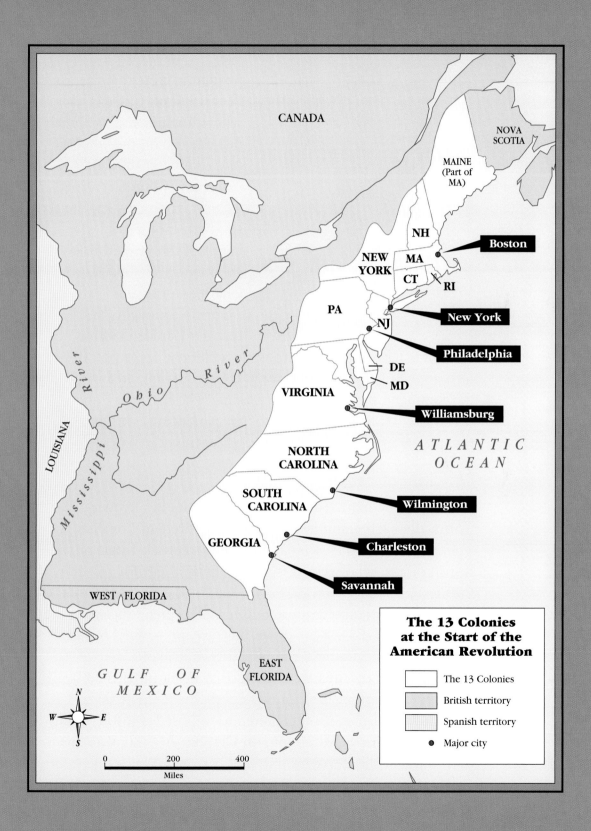

CANADA

NOVA SCOTIA

MAINE (Part of MA)

NH

NEW YORK

MA

Boston

CT

RI

PA

New York

NJ

Philadelphia

DE

MD

VIRGINIA

Williamsburg

ATLANTIC OCEAN

NORTH CAROLINA

SOUTH CAROLINA

Wilmington

GEORGIA

Charleston

Savannah

LOUISIANA

Mississippi River

Ohio River

WEST FLORIDA

EAST FLORIDA

GULF OF MEXICO

N
W E
S

0   200   400
Miles

The 13 Colonies at the Start of the American Revolution

☐ The 13 Colonies

▨ British territory

▨ Spanish territory

● Major city

British troops and cavalry under Cornwallis defeated the Americans under Gates at the Battle of Camden.

prisoners wrote that the force "consisted of ... young men whose apparel was extremely ragged, and on the whole ... looked greatly starved."

In June, Clinton returned to New York City, leaving the southern campaign in the hands of the veteran British commander General Lord Charles Cornwallis. By August, Cornwallis had reached Camden, South Carolina. There the British took on a colonial force of 4,000 men, mainly Patriot militia from the surrounding areas, under the command of General Henry Gates. The Battle of Camden was the worst loss of the war for the Americans, with more than 3,300 men killed, wounded, or captured.

"A Chain of Evils"

By the time he marched into North Carolina in October 1780, Cornwallis's left column was made up entirely of Loyalists. They were under the command of Major Patrick Ferguson, a British officer, who seemed to have a natural gift for recruiting men to fight under him. As the British force entered the area of Kings Mountain, Ferguson and his men spread the word that if the colonists did not lay down their weapons, the Loyalists would "lay the country waste with fire and sword."

Residents of the area were enraged at being threatened by their own countrymen. A Patriot militia made up of sharp-shooting woodsmen soon gathered to oppose Ferguson's unit. The Battle of Kings Mountain, on October 7, 1780, was the only battle of the Revolution fought between Americans.

After intense fighting, the Patriots killed Ferguson and soundly defeated the Loyalists. Ferguson was the only British officer killed in the battle. The rest were Americans—225 Loyalists and 28 Patriots.

Patriot riflemen defeated Loyalist Americans at the Battle of Kings Mountain.

The defeat at Kings Mountain forced Cornwallis to fall back into South Carolina. With the death of the popular Ferguson, the British never again successfully raised Loyalist militia. When Clinton received news of the defeat, he said he hoped that it was not "the first link in a chain of evils."

Clinton's fears were not unfounded. Cornwallis spent the last months of 1780 fighting off hit-and-run raids by Patriots such as the legendary "Swamp Fox," Francis Marion, who gained his nickname with his habit of vanishing into the thick Carolina swamps after missions.

The Road to Yorktown

As 1781 began, the British army controlled three of the major ports in America—New York; Charleston; and Savannah, Georgia. Inland, American forces held New England, the mid-Atlantic states, and Virginia. Neither side was closer to achieving victory than it had been the year before. The British did not have the manpower to push inland over the large area of the colonies, and the Americans did not have the firepower to drive the British out of the ports.

Patrick Ferguson

★ ★ ★ ★ ★

Patrick Ferguson was one of the most widely respected officers in the British army during the Revolution. Born in Scotland, he joined the army at 15 and distinguished himself during the Seven Years' War. His abilities as a marksman became legendary, and in 1774, he invented a breech-loading rifle—a weapon that could be loaded from the side rather than from the end of the barrel. British commanders were so impressed with the rifle that Ferguson was asked to demonstrate it for King George III. The Scottish marksman was able to fire between four and six shots per minute during a driving rain, and hit targets squarely at 200 yards—a performance far and above those achieved with the standard British musket.

When the Revolution began, Ferguson and a special sharpshooting unit—the Ferguson Rifles—fought under Clinton. In the unit's first action, at the Battle of Brandywine in 1777, Ferguson had an American officer in his sights, but refused to fire because the officer's back was turned. When his comrades asked why he did not fire, Ferguson replied, "It is ungentlemanly to shoot a man in the back of the head."

Ferguson later learned that the officer he had in his sights was George Washington.

Ferguson rifles were loaded from the side.

For Cornwallis, commander of the British southern campaign, the year began badly. In January, his force was defeated at the Battle of Cowpens, South Carolina, by an American force under regulars led by General Nathanael Greene and militia under General Daniel Morgan.

For the next three months, Greene led Cornwallis on a chase across North Carolina, and harassed him with raids that destroyed the spirit of the British regulars. Cornwallis, a man once called "the best soldier in the British army," was constantly outfoxed by Greene, his ragged regulars, and the buckskin-clad militiamen. In April, a frustrated Cornwallis wrote, "I am quite tired of marching about the country." To win the war, he wrote, "We must... bring our whole force into Virginia."

By that time, a sizable British force already in Virginia was causing serious trouble. As Cornwallis plodded through North Carolina, more than 3,000 British troops under General William Phillips and Arnold destroyed ships, docks, warehouses, and tobacco plantations in the eastern area of the state.

Jefferson was able to raise only a small militia force to defend the state and appealed to Washington for help. In response, Washington sent as many men as he could spare—about 1,200—to Virginia under the command of General Marie Joseph Paul Yves Roch Gilbert du Mortier, Marquis de Lafayette.

Lafayette was a 24-year-old Frenchman who had come to America three years before to volunteer his services.

ABOVE: Nathanael Greene commanded southern Patriots after the defeat at Camden.

BELOW: Lafayette became like a son to Washington during the Revolution.

15

Lafayette marched his force to Annapolis, Maryland, where the troops boarded boats, sailed down the Chesapeake Bay, and landed in Yorktown in March 1781. There they joined General Friedrich Wilhelm Augustus von Steuben. Von Steuben, a noble with the title of baron, was a Prussian officer who had drilled Washington's men into a disciplined fighting force during the terrible winter at Valley Forge. Von Steuben intended to accomplish the same task with the Virginia militia.

Throughout the spring, Lafayette's men attempted to keep the British bottled up in eastern Virginia. The British were able to do a great deal of damage in the port areas of the southeast, but the Americans prevented more widespread attacks.

In May, Cornwallis crossed into Virginia and joined forces with Arnold, now in sole command of the British force there. The British had some 8,000 well-armed troops in the state against Lafayette's force of 1,200 regulars, 900 militia, and six cannons. A face-to-face battle, therefore, was out of the question for the Americans. They were reduced to shadowing the British army and occasionally engaging in skirmishes.

As events unfolded in Virginia through the spring of 1781, Washington and Rochambeau met for the second time in May in Wethersfield, Connecticut. Washington still felt that their main objective should be an attack on the British stronghold in New York City. Rochambeau, however, supported the strategy of sending troops south if favorable conditions arose there.

Favorable conditions soon did arise. In mid-June, a letter from Washington to Lafayette was intercepted by the British. In the letter, Washington revealed his plan to invade New York City. In response, Clinton immediately ordered Cornwallis to march east from his location near Richmond to a port area near Williamsburg. From there, he was to send half his force back to New York City by ship. Arnold was recalled to the city to aid in its defense.

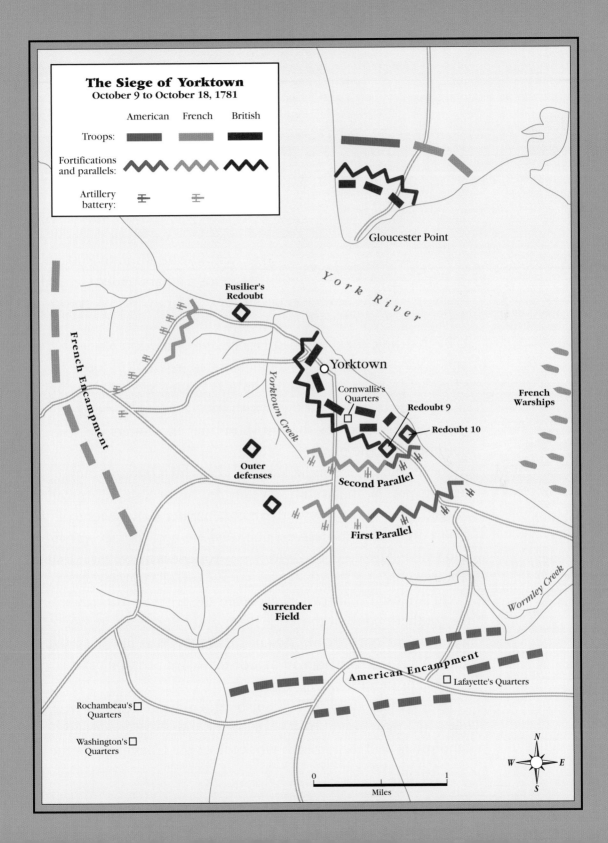

The Siege of Yorktown
October 9 to October 18, 1781

Troops: American French British

Fortifications and parallels:

Artillery battery:

Gloucester Point

York River

Fusilier's Redoubt

French Encampment

Yorktown

Cornwallis's Quarters

Redoubt 9

Redoubt 10

French Warships

Outer defenses

Second Parallel

First Parallel

Wormley Creek

Yorktown Creek

Surrender Field

American Encampment

Lafayette's Quarters

Rochambeau's Quarters

Washington's Quarters

N
W E
S

0   1
Miles

New York City was a British stronghold during the Revolution.

This order forced the large British force onto a narrow peninsula of land between the James and York Rivers. Although this was a vulnerable position, Cornwallis was not concerned, because his force was several times larger than the American force, even with the addition of 800 more regulars under General Anthony Wayne. Several times in June and July, British troops defeated colonials in skirmishes and ambushes.

By mid-July, the combined French and American forces under Washington and Rochambeau had assembled north of Manhattan. Even so, Washington was having second thoughts about a direct attack on the British stronghold. His men had been easily stopped by the British in brief encounters at outposts over the previous weeks.

For his part, Clinton had second thoughts about needing reinforcements. In late July, he canceled his order to Cornwallis. Instead, he ordered the southern commander to take control of a port area that was deep enough to allow both British warships and troop ships to dock. With New York secure, he would send troops to begin a British campaign to control Virginia.

On August 1, Cornwallis occupied the ports of Yorktown on the southern bank of the York River and Gloucester, across the water on the north bank. Again, Cornwallis was unconcerned about locating his troops in a poor defensive position. The Americans did not worry him.

Twelve miles away in Williamsburg, Lafayette realized that under the right conditions—sufficient numbers of troops and cannons as well as a French blockade of the Chesapeake—the

American forces could actually defeat the mighty British army. In early August, Lafayette sent a messenger to Washington with the news of Cornwallis's move.

At the same time, Washington received encouraging information. A French fleet of 34 warships and more than 3,000 troops under Comte de Grasse had set sail from the West Indies several weeks earlier. They planned to reach the Chesapeake Bay in early September.

On August 14, Washington made his decision. The French and American force, more than 8,000 men, would march as quickly as possible to engage Cornwallis at Yorktown. They broke camp on August 17, but they left behind a small force stationed around New York City to create the impression that they still planned an attack. This move fooled Clinton briefly and delayed his plans to send troops south.

Comte de Grasse had been in the French navy for almost 40 years before the Revolution.

The Americans and the French marched 25 to 30 miles a day and reached Philadelphia by September 1. On September 5, de Grasse's French fleet defeated a British fleet under Admiral Thomas Graves at the mouth of the Chesapeake Bay in an engagement known as the Battle of the Capes. As the allied armies headed south, the French navy blockaded the York River.

By September 17, the combined American and French force had reached Annapolis. Troops boarded transports for the trip down the Chesapeake Bay to Williamsburg, where they met up with the men under Lafayette, Wayne, and von Steuben. Supply wagons, artillery, and cavalry continued south by land.

On September 28, British troops in defensive positions around Yorktown heard the unmistakable sounds of thousands of marching feet. They were surrounded by a force of nearly 15,000 soldiers on one side, the York River on the other, and a French fleet that stood in the way of escape.

"Great Shellfish Bay"

★ ★ ★ ★ ★

The first white men to explore the Atlantic Coast in the mid-1500s discovered thousands of natives living around an enormous estuary—a body of

Sailing on the Chesapeake Bay cut weeks over travel on land during colonial times.

mixed salt and freshwater—that the natives called Chesepioc—"great shellfish bay." As Europeans settled in America, the Chesapeake Bay became one of the most important water highways in the colonies. The first African slaves to come to America sailed into Chesapeake Bay in 1619. The first tobacco and cotton crops sailed out of the bay at about the same time. During the final military campaign of the Revolution, travel on the waters of the Chesapeake cut weeks off of the journey between New York and Virginia and allowed forces to converge with almost perfect timing.

The Chesapeake Bay is about 200 miles long, with its northern end at Havre de Grace, Maryland, and its mouth at Norfolk, Virginia. It varies in width from about three miles in the north to 35 miles wide near the mouth of the Potomac River. Along that entire length, it receives the waters of 150 major rivers and more than 100,000 streams. Its 11,684 miles of shoreline are more than the entire West Coast of the United States.

Although the bay is large, it is relatively shallow, with an average depth of about 21 feet. For that reason, Washington and Rochambeau were unable to ship the heavy supply wagons and livestock to Yorktown by water. Such heavy loads would have bottomed out any boat.

The Final Siege

By late September, clouds of mosquitoes and unclean living conditions among the British at Yorktown had spread malaria, typhoid fever, and smallpox among the troops. After nearly two months encamped in Yorktown, more than 3,000 troops—from Cornwallis's total force of 8,000—were ill. This delayed the British in digging defensive fortifications.

Cornwallis himself continued to cling to the hope that reinforcements from New York would arrive. When the news that the French had blockaded the York River reached his headquarters, however, he set the troops to work digging defensive fortifications with new urgency. The effort was aided by more than 2,000 African American slaves who had fled to Yorktown after an offer was spread throughout the region offering freedom in return for aiding the British.

Washington and Rochambeau believed that a siege would defeat British forces.

The defenses the British constructed were essentially two curved lines of trenches for troops. These ditches—about four feet deep and seven feet wide—were interspersed with redoubts, raised earthen forts, supported by logs, that served as artillery positions. Around the raised earthworks were abatis, barricades of sharp-edged branches.

The first line, called the inner defense, was about 1.5 miles long and constructed closest to Yorktown. The outer defense line, further from the town, partially blocked the main road from Williamsburg. This line had three well-armed redoubts built on the western and eastern ends of the line, near the York River. They were called the Fusilier's Redoubt, Redoubt 9, and Redoubt 10.

21

By that time, Cornwallis had also established a camp across the York River at Gloucester Point. That position, however, was lightly defended. Washington sent a small militia force to that camp to close off any escape routes.

After they scouted the location, the French and American officers were convinced that the battle for Yorktown would be a siege—an attack in which one army surrounds an enemy location and bombards it with artillery. Because the artillery was still several days away, the first part of the allied plan called for digging trenches and constructing redoubts several hundred yards from the outer defense of the British.

As events progressed, Washington realized how important the battle had become. By several strokes of luck—and French assistance—the Americans suddenly found themselves in position to defeat a force that was almost one-third of the entire British army in America. To impress that fact on his men, Washington sent a message among the troops, telling them "the present moment will decide American independence."

On October 6, as the Americans completed work on their position, a heavy rain turned the trenches into muddy holes. Nevertheless, Washington ordered his troops to work day and night to complete a large raised earthwork. Working in wet, humid, and muddy conditions, the allies created a 2,000-foot-long parallel—also called a siege line—less a half mile from the British lines. Dozens of platforms were built, and more than 100 cannons were dragged into place. By the morning of October 9, the 16-man gun crews were ready for action, and the trenches bristled with the muskets of French and American troops.

The Shooting Begins

At 3 o'clock on the afternoon of October 9, the French artillery opened fire. When American artillery began firing two hours later, Washington himself fired the first cannon. The Battle of

Yorktown was the only battle of the war that was fought almost entirely with artillery.

Shooting mainly 12- and 18-pound cannon-balls and canister shot, the cannons fired around the clock. Even though a cannon could not be fired more than once an hour or the barrel would melt, there were enough big guns to fire more than 1,700 shots a day—about one every 80 seconds—against the British. The effect was devastating. Cornwallis was forced to evacuate the home he had taken for headquarters when cannon fire began to hit it. The general took cover in an earthen bunker behind the house.

American cannons could only be fired once an hour or their barrels would melt.

Cornwallis soon found the combined fire of several hundred French and American guns much fiercer than the small numbers of American artillery he had previously encountered in open battle. "The fire continued . . . until all our guns on the left were silenced . . . and our loss of men considerable," he wrote.

A British officer wrote that the bombardment was "one continual roar of cannon, mixed with the bursting of shells and rumbling of houses torn to pieces." A soldier in the trenches wrote that he "saw men lying everywhere who were mortally wounded and whose heads, arms, and legs had been shot off."

On October 11, Washington ordered his force to move closer to construct a second parallel closer to Yorktown, which would tighten their ring against the enemy. Work began, but enemy fire from Redoubts 9 and 10 on the eastern end of the British defense drove the troops back. Allied artillery was unable to dislodge the gunners and riflemen, and Washington was stopped.

23

British Generals: Clinton and Cornwallis

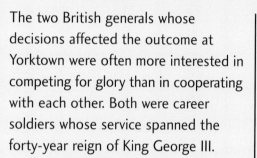

The two British generals whose decisions affected the outcome at Yorktown were often more interested in competing for glory than in cooperating with each other. Both were career soldiers whose service spanned the forty-year reign of King George III.

Sir Henry Clinton was born in Canada in 1730 and grew up in New York, where his father served as royal governor for several years. Clinton joined the army in 1751 and served in the French and Indian Wars. In 1772, his wife died after five years of marriage, and her death deeply affected Clinton. He became withdrawn and often argued with his fellow officers over minor matters.

In 1778, Clinton became the commander of British armies in America and located his command in the British stronghold of New York City.

Finally, after three days, Washington ordered the redoubts to be stormed. Each would be attacked by a force of 400 infantrymen. Washington first sent men with axes to cut paths through the abatis. An iron storm of musket balls whizzed past the attackers as they cut through the barricades, but defensive fire from the French finally allowed the job to be completed.

His greatest military triumph during the Revolution was the victory at Charleston, South Carolina, a battle in which almost the entire American navy was wiped out in the city's harbor.

Clinton arrived in England in 1782 to learn that he was held responsible for the defeat at Yorktown. He wrote a book that described the events from his point of view, and shifted much of the blame to Cornwallis. Clinton died in 1795 while serving as governor of the British colony of Gibraltar.

Lord Charles Cornwallis was born into nobility in 1738. Although he was blinded in one eye from a childhood game, he was accepted into the British army at age 18. As a young man he served in Parliament, where he consistently voted against the tax acts that the colonists also opposed.

Cornwallis served during the Revolution under both William Howe and Clinton, and saw action in New York, New Jersey, and Pennsylvania. He faced Washington before Yorktown in several key battles, including Princeton, Brandywine, and Monmouth. After the war, Cornwallis continued military service to the Crown in both Ireland and India. He died in India in 1805.

Sir Henry Clinton was an unpopular commander.

After the paths were cleared, American soldiers led by Colonel Alexander Hamilton—later the first secretary of the treasury—stormed Redoubt 10. French soldiers, and a unit of African American soldiers from Rhode Island, under Colonel Marshal du Houx de Viomenil, attempted to take Redoubt 9. The fighting was mostly hand-to-hand with swords and bayonets.

Washington fired the first American artillery shot of the siege.

Eventually, at the cost of 25 American and French soldiers, the British soldiers were forced off the redoubts. As soon as the redoubts were in American and French control, they were linked to the second parallel and artillery was positioned at even closer range.

On October 15, Cornwallis sent a message to Clinton. The commander had been in enough battles to know that his situation was almost hopeless. "Our fresh earthen works do not resist their powerful artillery, so that we shall soon be exposed to an assault in ruined works...with weakened numbers," he wrote. "I cannot recommend that the fleet and army...risque [risk]...endeavoring to save us."

On October 16, a group of officers appealed to Cornwallis, as he wrote later, "to evacuate the miserable works of Yorktown; where every hour both by day and night, was an hour of watching and danger to the officer and soldier." His fierce and trusted officer, cavalry commander Banastre Tarlton, told Cornwallis that "a retreat by Gloucester is the only expedient... to avert...a surrender."

Thus, Cornwallis made the decision on the evening of October 16 to remove his infantry across the York River to Gloucester Point. There, against a lighter defense, he reasoned, the troops might break through and retreat northward toward New York. Cornwallis ordered more than 2,000 soldiers into a fleet of small wooden boats. He left his sick and wounded— and his heavy guns—behind.

While the first wave of soldiers crossed the dark water, Cornwallis prepared to lead the second group across. Suddenly

The Battle of Yorktown

a vicious rain and lightning storm arose. In the driving wind and rain, two boatloads of soldiers were pushed helplessly down the York into the arms of the French navy. The plan was then canceled.

The men who made it across had little better luck. They returned to Yorktown on the morning of October 17, and told Cornwallis that the American defense was firmly entrenched. "Nothing passes in or out," reported one officer. Cornwallis knew then that his hours in command were numbered.

The Surrender at Yorktown

After he inspected what was left of his defensive line, Cornwallis decided that "it would have been inhuman to . . . sacrifice the lives of this small body of gallant soldiers." He called a young drummer forward to play a drumroll, the signal for a meeting. A British officer followed the drummer, and waved a white flag. The officer, who carried a message from Cornwallis, was blindfolded and taken to Washington.

The meetings between officers of both sides lasted two days. At first, Cornwallis wanted Washington to allow his troops to return to England with the promise that they would not return to the war. Washington refused. Although he offered terms that

Cornwallis claimed he was sick and did not actually participate in the surrender on October 19.

The Battle of Yorktown

French Officers: Rochambeau and DeGrasse

⭐ ⭐ ⭐ ⭐ ⭐

Although Marquis de Lafayette is well known for his role in the American Revolution, the parts played by two career French officers led to the victory at Yorktown. Without these two men, one a general, the other an admiral, the victory might never have occurred.

Comte de Rochambeau was born into nobility in 1725. His full name was Jean-Baptist-Donatien de Vimeur, Comte de Rochambeau. He abandoned his original plans to become a priest and entered military service in 1741. He quickly rose through the ranks and became a commander respected both by his superiors and the men who fought under him.

King Louis XVI sent Rochambeau to America in 1780 in command of the first French troops to aid the United States. Rochambeau was astonished at the terrible condition of the American

would allow British officers to keep their weapons and return to England with Cornwallis, he insisted that the troops would be held as prisoners until the end of the war.

At midnight on October 19, Washington sent his terms to Cornwallis with orders that the agreement be signed by 11 o'clock. The agreement stated that the ceremony of surrender would

army and thus was cautious about engaging the British in New York City. Throughout his meetings and communications with Washington, he continued to urge the American commander to consider focusing efforts on the Chesapeake Bay region. When Cornwallis surrendered, Rochambeau was presented with one of the captured British cannons.

Rochambeau returned to France after the war, where he was almost beheaded during the revolution there. He died in France in 1807.

Comte de Grasse, whose full name was François Joseph Paul, Marquis de Grasse-Tilly, was born in 1722 and became a naval cadet at age 11. Thus by the time the American Revolution began, de Grasse had been in the French navy for more than 40 years.

A large man, well over six feet tall, he was said to be so furiously intense in battle that he changed into a monster.

His one great contribution to the American Revolution, the victory in the Battle of the Capes in September 1781, was the key to the later success at Yorktown. Washington himself called de Grasse "the Arbitrator [one who decides] of the War."

Soon after the Battle of Yorktown, de Grasse's fleet was defeated by the British in the West Indies. De Grasse was taken prisoner and sent to London. After the war, he remained in London to help work out the details of the peace treaty between France, England, and the United States. He died shortly after he returned to France in 1788. Today there is a street named for de Grasse in Yorktown.

begin with the British marching out "at two o'clock precisely with shouldered arms . . . and drums beating. They are then to ground [give up] their arms and return to their encampments . . . until they are dispatched to their places of destination."

At precisely 2 o'clock on October 19, 1781, the British soldiers, wearing their famous red coats, passed between two

29

lines of French and American soldiers. The French were dressed in bright, well-tailored blue uniforms. Washington and his officers were dressed in blue jackets and white pants. The American troops were dressed as they had been for much of the war. In the words of a French officer, the Americans "were clad in small jackets of white cloth, dirty and ragged, and a number of them were almost barefoot."

Epilogue

When the prime minister of England received word of the defeat at Yorktown a month after the surrender, he said, "Oh, God! It is all over." In fact, the war did not officially end for two more years, when the Treaty of Paris was signed in 1783. After Yorktown, however, no more large-scale battles were fought between the Americans and the British.

Throughout the Revolution, George Washington showed himself again and again to be a man of rare courage under the most discouraging circumstances. Yet even he realized that victory at Yorktown was due more to circumstance than courage.

In a time when communications traveled by foot, by hoof, or by sail, he was able to coordinate the movements of a French army in Rhode Island, a Frenchman commanding Americans in Virginia, and a French fleet in the West Indies. Somehow, these forces came together at the right place and right time to find the mighty British army in a weak position. Then, when the redcoats attempted to escape from their corner, a storm arrived to wash away their hope.

Years later, Washington wrote that his victory at Yorktown was due largely to "the interposing hand of Heaven."

Washington was grateful for his good fortune at Yorktown.

Glossary

abatis defensive wall made of sharpened poles

artillery cannons, mortars, and other heavy guns used in the military

commission the appointment of an officer to a high rank in the armies and navies of the eighteenth century

Loyalist American colonist who remained loyal to the king of England during the American Revolution, also called Tory

militia citizen armed forces that fought the British

Parliament legislative branch of English government, consisting of the House of Commons and the House of Lords

Patriot one who resisted the British in America

redcoats British soldiers who wore bright red field jackets

redoubt a raised artillery emplacement

reinforcements fresh soldiers sent to strengthen a military unit

siege the surrounding and blockading of a city, town, or fortress by an army attempting to capture it

skirmishes minor or preliminary conflicts or disputes

For More Information

Books

Ferrie, Richard. *The World Turned Upside Down*. New York: Holiday House, 1999.

Weber, Michael. *Yorktown* (Battlefields Across America). Breckinridge, CO: Twenty-First Century Books, 1997.

Web Sites

Liberty! The American Revolution
http://www.pbs.org/ktca/liberty/
Good overview of events leading the war.

The Yorktown Campaign
http://xenophongroup.com/mcjoynt/yrkcam-z.htm
Excellent resource with detailed timeline.

The Patriot Resource
http://www.patriotresource.com/people/cornwallis.html
Good biographical material and timeline.

Index

The Battle of Yorktown